A DORLING KINDERSLEY BOOK

Note to Parents

My First Look At Things That Go is designed to help young children
learn about different kinds of vehicles and toys – whether they move on the road,
on tracks, through water, or in the air. It's a book for you and your child to share
and enjoy – looking at the pages together, finding familiar objects,
and learning and using new words.

Editors Andrea Pinnington,
Charlotte Davies
Designer Heather Blackham
Managing Editor Jane Yorke

Senior Art Editor Mark Richards
Photography Steve Gorton
Series Consultant Neil Morris

Dorling Kindersley would like to thank John Bennett of Eltham Models
for the loan of the model ships and boats.

First published in Great Britain in 1991
by Dorling Kindersley Limited,
9 Henrietta Street, London WC2E 8PS
Reprinted 1991, 1994
Copyright © 1991 Dorling Kindersley Limited, London

A CIP catalogue record for this book is available from the British Library.

ISBN 0-86318-608-4

Reproduced by Bright Arts, Hong Kong
Printed and bound in Italy by L.E.G.O.

· MY · FIRST · LOOK · AT ·

Things that go

DK
DORLING KINDERSLEY
London · New York · Stuttgart

On the road

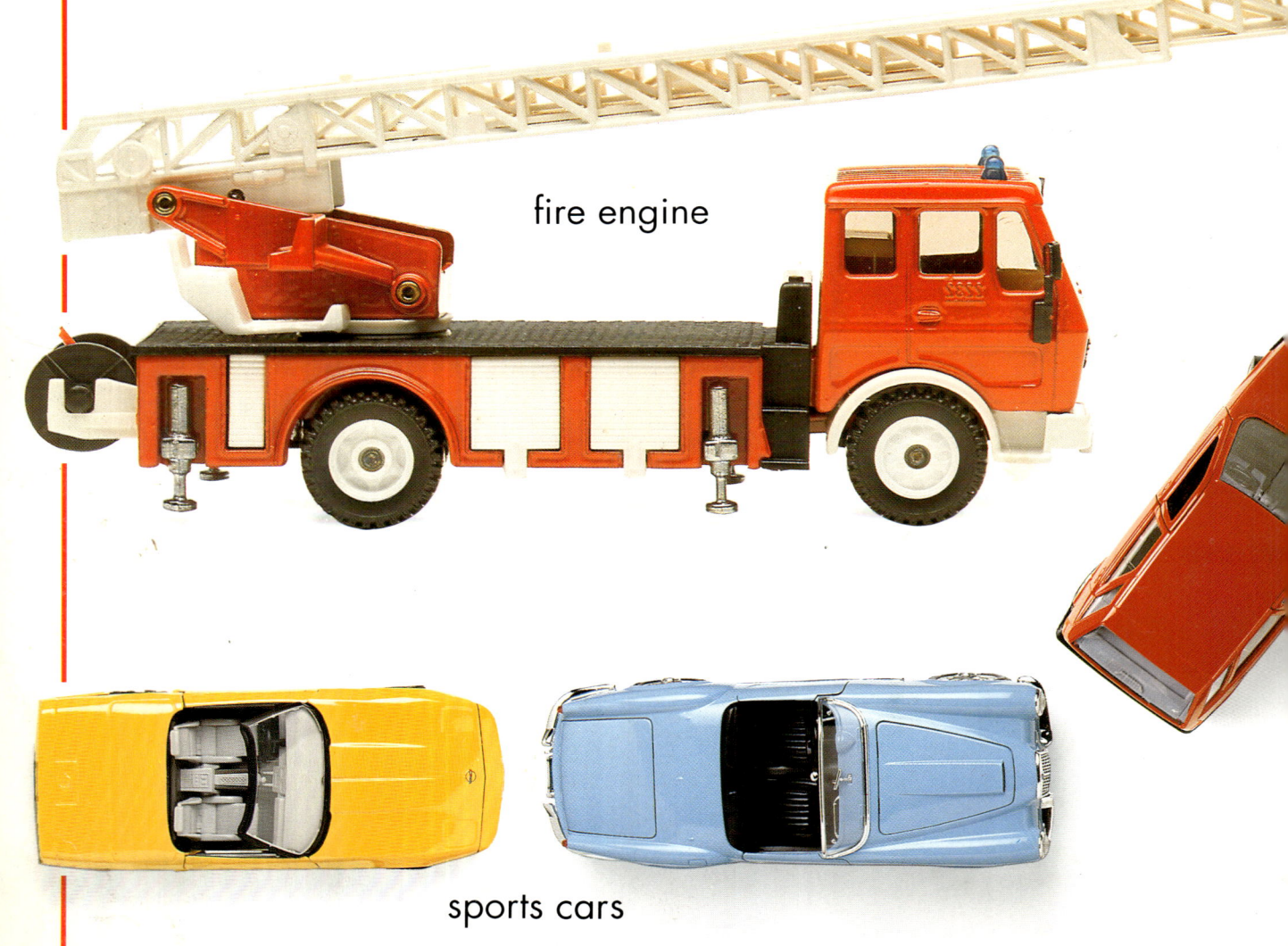

fire engine

sports cars

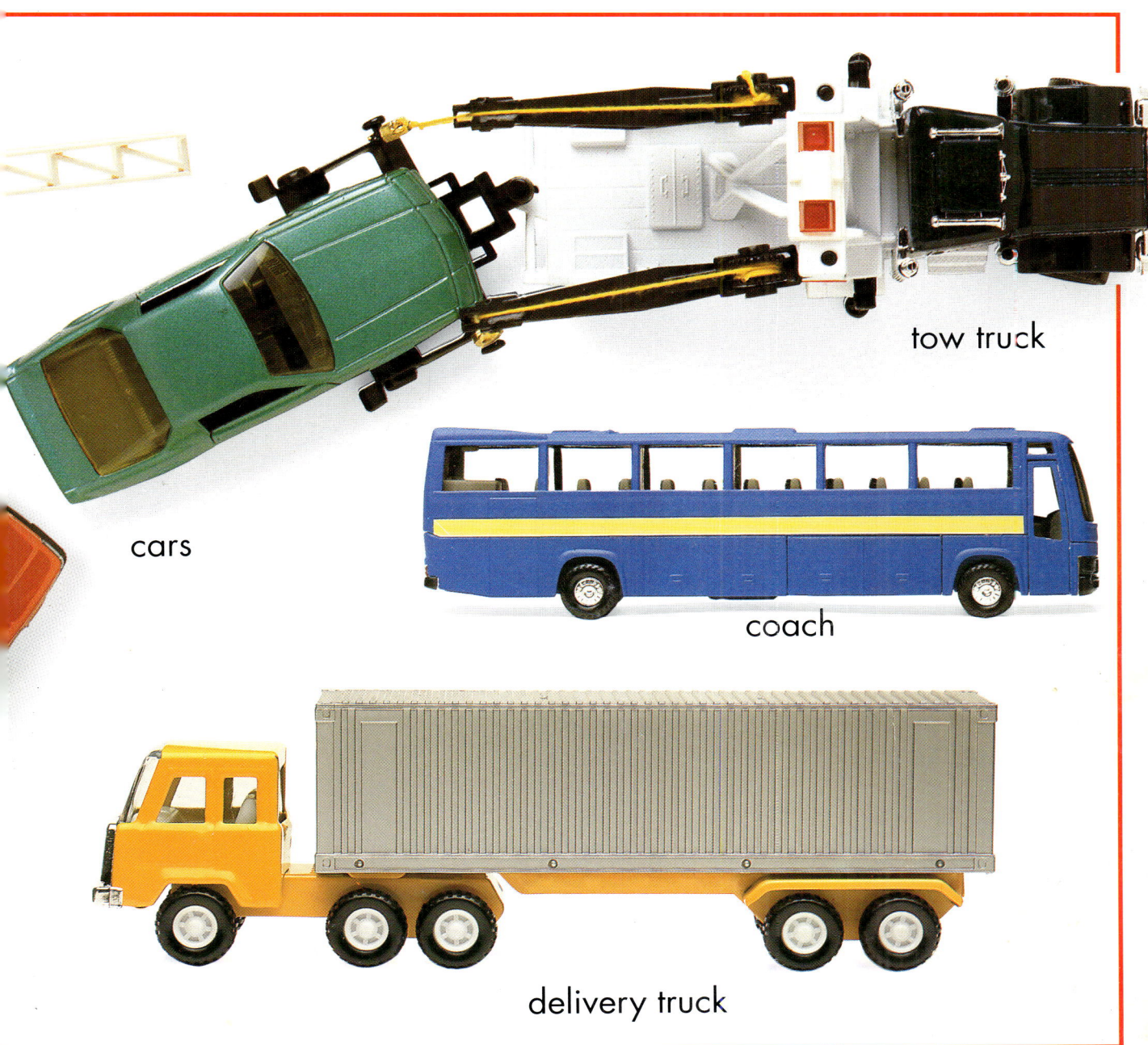

tow truck

cars

coach

delivery truck

3

Toys that go

skateboard

pull-along frog

scooter

sledge

4

truck

roller-skates

tricycle

stroller

5

On tracks

steam engine

wagons

passenger train

locomotive

On the building site

bulldozer

digger

concrete mixer

dumper truck

9

On the farm

horse trailer

jeep

tractor

trailer

combine
harvester

plough

In the air

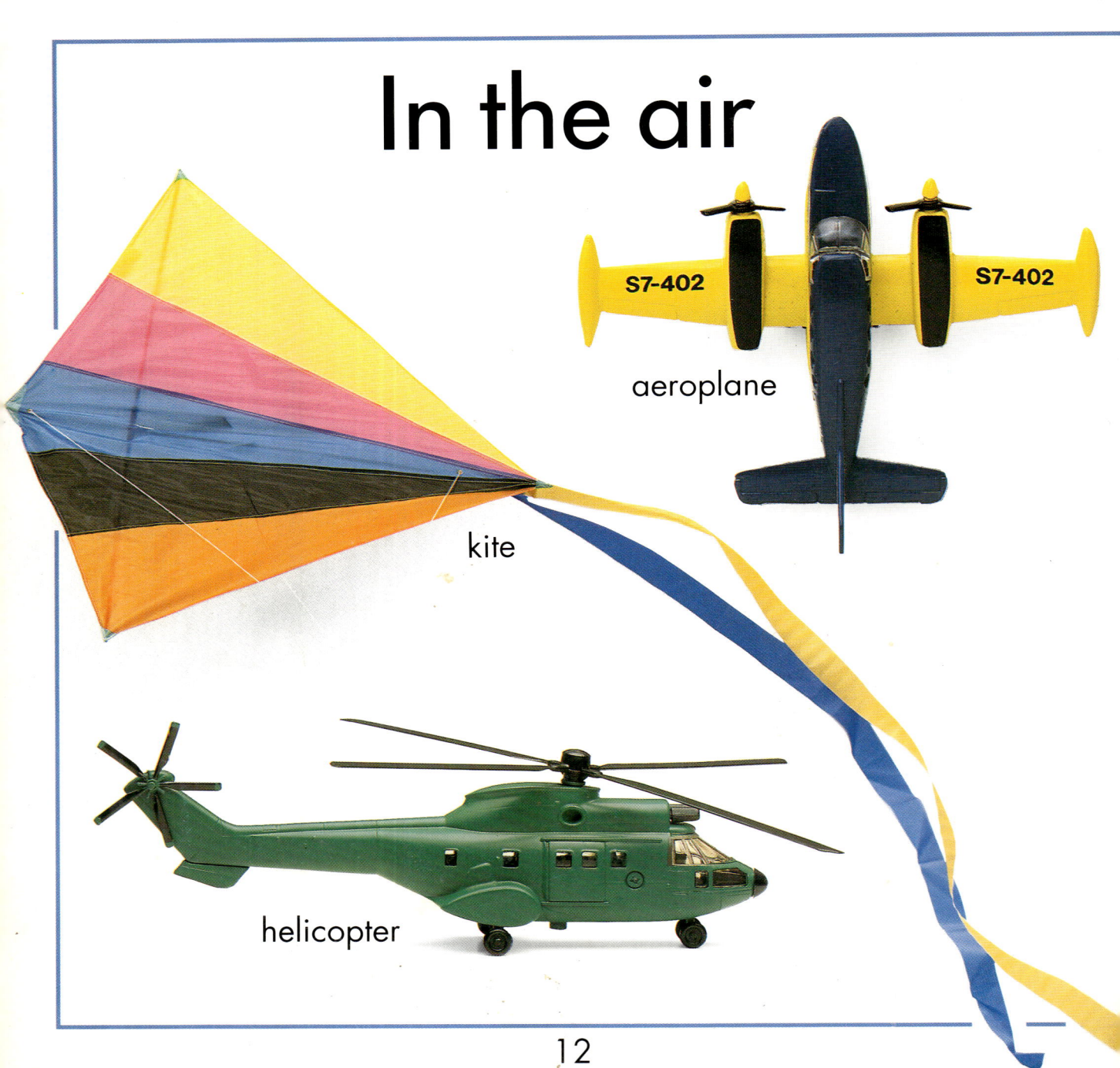

aeroplane

kite

helicopter

passenger
plane

balloons

space shuttle

13

In the water

tug boat

bath toys

submarine

fishing boat

E 650

motor boat

sailing boat

15

Things that go fast

speedboat

racing car

motorbike

Things that go slow

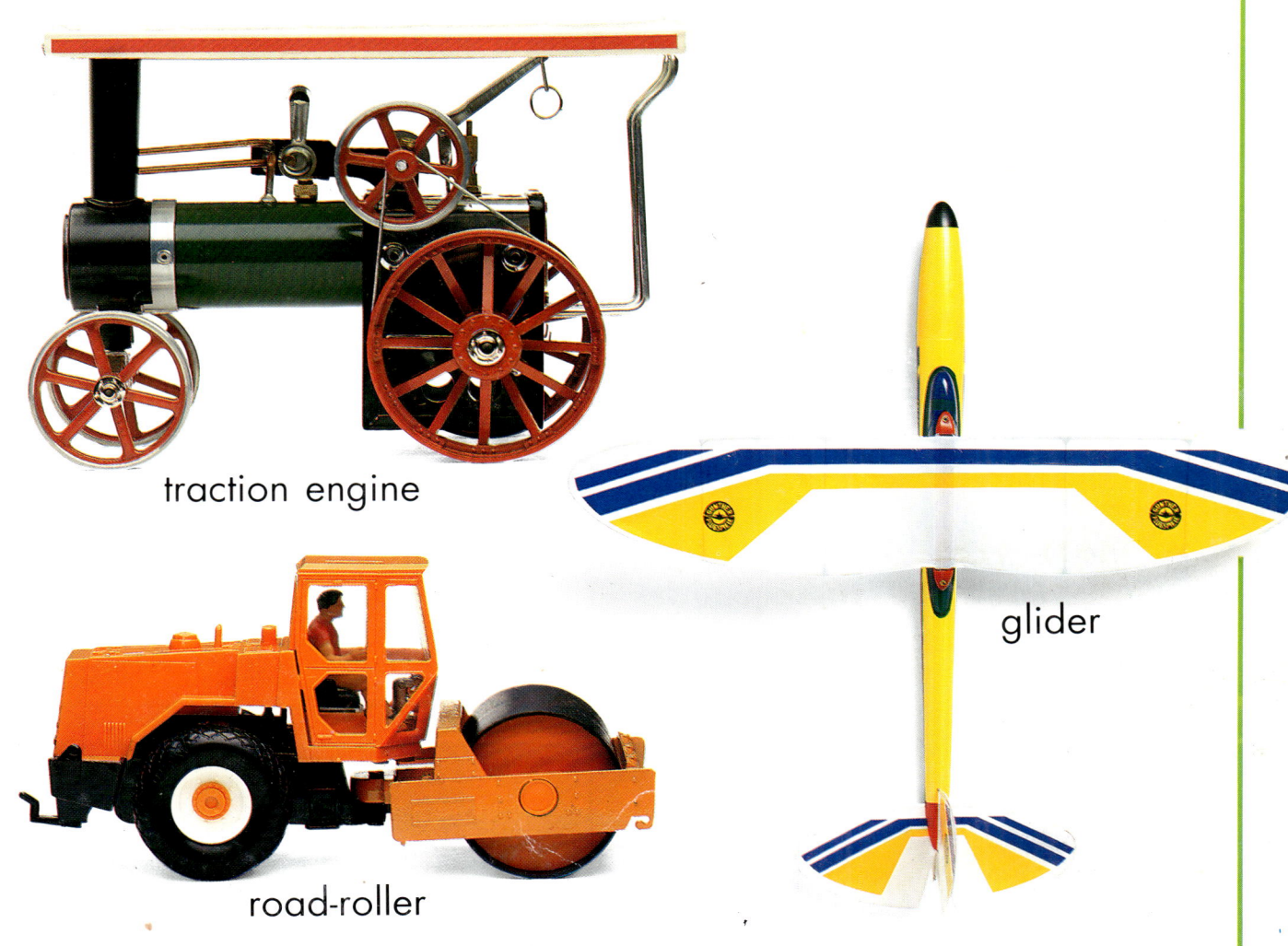

traction engine

road-roller

glider